A New Fourth Step Guide

INTRODUCTION

In 1960, Hazelden introduced its *Guide to Fourth Step Inventory* to assist alcoholics in taking their personal inventories. A few years later, it developed the *Guide to Fourth Step Inventory For the Spouse* to assist family members in taking their own inventories.

Both of these Guides quickly became very popular and are now widely used throughout the country not only by A.A. and Al-Anon members, but by members of Overeaters Anonymous, Families Anonymous, Neurotics Anonymous, Narcotics Anonymous and a host of other self-help groups, as well as hundreds of treatment centers and hospitals with alcoholism and drug dependency units.

Out of this background and experience has grown this *New Fourth Step Guide*. Our original *Fourth Step Guides* will remain in print for those who find them preferable.

Tenth Printing, 1981

ISBN: 0-89486-000-3

Hazelden Foundation

Printed in the United States of America.

INSTRUCTIONS FOR USE OF THE NEW FOURTH STEP GUIDE

Step Four (like each of the Steps) marks the beginning of a new way of life. It says that today I will begin to take a realistic assessment of myself. We hope this guide will help you begin to learn to know yourself.

Three attitudes are important: To be searching, fearless and moral.

1. Are you searching? Are you really digging into your own self-awareness and describing your behavior as it really is?

2. Are you fearless? It takes courage to face yourself in terms of what has really been going on in your life.

3. Are you moral? Take a good look at the "good-bad" implications of your behavior. How does it size up with your own values?

Take a searching, fearless and moral inventory, but don't be moralistic. You know your behavior has good and bad aspects. That is a fact of life. Look at it. Own your own behavior. But don't punish yourself. Our goal is to know ourselves and to accept ourselves. Only then can we begin to change and grow.

Give examples of your behavior that specifically describe your reality. Put this in writing, in black and white, on paper, with specific searching and fearless examples.

Many have found it helpful to reserve a special section for facing things they have never shared before, the "what-bugs-me-most" behavior, what they least like to face in themselves, what they would find difficult to share with another person.

The Fourth Step is a simple and direct beginning to an on-going task of life, a direction to walk toward self-awareness, a way to go today and each day from now on. The moral inventory becomes a way of life based on the courage to be honest with ourselves.

You may experience some distress while writing the Fourth Step. This is normal. You may find yourself growing resentful, becoming depressed, feeling guilty, afraid of failure. You may find yourself putting off the job until tomorrow! Share these thoughts and feelings with your counselor or chaplain, and make what you discover about yourself part of your inventory.

This self-assessment may very well be the most courageous act of your life. If you need encouragement, support and help, ask for it!

FALSE PRIDE

What we mean is excessive pride; being so thin-skinned that we have trouble admitting any human weaknesses at all. Another word for this kind of pride is grandiosity. Describe how your pride has kept you from looking at your own behavior.

WRITE SPECIFIC EXAMPLES

HUMILITY

Now that you are learning that it is safe to admit your powerlessness and unmanageability, do you find it easier just to be human? Being humble doesn't mean being weak. It means accepting ourselves — our strengths as well as our weaknesses. Do you know something now about what humility really means? Are you able to be less defensive? To enjoy the peace that comes with genuine humility? Explain.

WRITE SPECIFIC EXAMPLES

PERFECTIONISM

Too often we are unwilling to accept human mistakes; our own or those of others. When we are afraid of criticism, we set unrealistic standards for ourselves, and we are frustrated if we can't meet them. When we're feeling this way, we are impatient with family members and friends and co-workers when they are imperfect, too. How has your need to be perfect hurt you? How have you made others unhappy by insisting that they be perfect, too?

WRITE SPECIFIC EXAMPLES

ADMITTING MISTAKES

Most of us have not had much experience in admitting mistakes and admitting when we are wrong. We seem to give ourselves only two choices: being absolutely perfect, or being totally worthless. What a relief it is when we can admit mistakes — admit we're human. Can you think of examples of your being in the wrong and admitting it? Is it OK to make mistakes?

WRITE SPECIFIC EXAMPLES

BEING PHONY

Being phony, conning, becomes part of our way of life when we are not being honest. We seem to have to look good to others, and being ourselves just doesn't seem to be enough sometimes. How have you been phony in the past? How are you being phony right now?

WRITE SPECIFIC EXAMPLES

BEING YOURSELF

Today you're doing something important: you're being honest and responsible. At last, you're just being yourself. Doesn't it feel good? Are you giving yourself enough credit for this? Giving yourself a pat on the back? How does your new feeling about yourself affect your relationships with others?

WRITE SPECIFIC EXAMPLES

SELFISHNESS

"I want what I want when I want it." Think about that. Do you spend a lot of time worrying about your own needs? Maybe you don't get what you want. But what about all the energy you put into trying, one way or another, to please yourself, to get your own way? How have you hurt others by putting your own needs first?

WRITE SPECIFIC EXAMPLES

SHARING

When we're feeling good about ourselves, we begin to care about the welfare and happiness of others, too. Have you learned how to hear other people, to see them, to know them? Do you know how to respond to the needs of others? To give of yourself? Have you learned how to share with others, to care about them? How does it feel?

WRITE SPECIFIC EXAMPLES

IMPATIENCE

When impatience gets the better of us, not only do we want what we want, but we want it right now. When we're feeling like this, and things don't work out the way they should, and on just the timetable we set, our blood pressure rises and we can be really miserable. Describe some situations in which your impatience caused damage to you — to others. How does your impatience get in your way right now?

WRITE SPECIFIC EXAMPLES

PATIENCE

Patience is an elusive goal: it's something we need to work on daily. Maybe we will never become truly patient people, but it is vital that we are not driven constantly by our impatience. As you work on your problems with perfectionism, do you find that you are more patient with yourself and with others? Are you learning how to take it easy?

WRITE SPECIFIC EXAMPLES

SELF-PITY

This is hard to recognize, and it's something no one likes to admit. It's a matter of feeling sorry for ourselves. Maybe because we feel people just don't understand us. Or maybe it's feeling that people don't respect us or don't love us enough. It means feeling hopeless, feeling like a victim of circumstances. Have you ever felt self-pity? Do you feel sorry for yourself right now?

WRITE SPECIFIC EXAMPLES

FEELING GOOD ABOUT YOURSELF

When we are working toward personal growth,we can begin to see the true meaning of "Love thy neighbor as thyself." It doesn't mean "more than" and it doesn't mean "less than." If we're able to respect ourselves, we are able to give love to others, and that's a basic part of feeling worthwhile. Are you able to see yourself as being worthwhile? Able to feel good about yourself? Try to illustrate this feeling with examples from your recent experience.

WRITE SPECIFIC EXAMPLES

RESENTMENT

Resentful people hang onto angry feelings. Angry feelings about our families. Angry feelings about how we live and where and when. Hanging onto bad feelings can really make us miserable. Resentments are always good excuses for our irresponsible behavior. Talk about resentments you have right now. Do you hang onto angry feelings because you think your anger is justified?

WRITE SPECIFIC EXAMPLES

FORGIVENESS AND UNDERSTANDING

Learning how to accept situations we cannot change and how to understand those people we think have wronged us are marks of personal growth. What do you know about forgiveness and understanding? Has the ability to accept the things you cannot change become a part of your life now?

WRITE SPECIFIC EXAMPLES

INTOLERANCE

Intolerance can grow from self-pity and resentment. Once we learn how, it becomes easy to blame others for the way we feel. Being intolerant is especially easy when others have different ways of thinking or living. However, it's also easy to be intolerant of those people who are close to us and who are important in our personal lives. How were you intolerant of others in the past? Think hard about this one: Are you still intolerant of others?

WRITE SPECIFIC EXAMPLES

TOLERANCE

As you learn to accept responsibility for your own feelings, do you find that you are more tolerant? Tolerant of yourself? Tolerant of others? Are you able to see the needs of others more clearly and to accept people as fellow human beings? To understand them? Are you able to accept yourself now?

WRITE SPECIFIC EXAMPLES

ALIBIS

How much have we invested in justifying our behavior to others by explaining for ourselves? Sometimes the explanations are true, sometimes they're partly true, often they're purely fiction. Can you think of ways you alibied for yourself? How did you feel about yourself when you did alibi? Do you catch yourself making up alibis now?

WRITE SPECIFIC EXAMPLES

BEING HONEST

What do you think of yourself now that you're trying to be open and honest? Do you feel more comfortable? Is it easier to be with other people? Is it a relief, not having to explain for yourself?

WRITE SPECIFIC EXAMPLES

DISHONEST THINKING

This happens when we begin making alibis to ourselves and believing them. When we really begin to believe our resentments. When we actually feel abused and misunderstood. The danger is that we will lose all contact with reality. How were you deceiving yourself in the past? How could you deceive yourself now about important matters in your life?

WRITE SPECIFIC EXAMPLES

HONEST THINKING

Being honest with ourselves is the most difficult form of honesty. As we learn how to accept ourselves as we really are, we can begin to laugh at ourselves for sometimes trying to be something else. Are you able to laugh at yourself in this way now?

WRITE SPECIFIC EXAMPLES

PUTTING THINGS OFF

Often, we put things off until we get the right inspiration, until everything is just right. And the right time almost never comes. When pressure builds to get a job done, we tend to react by becoming difficult to get along with — by becoming impatient and irresponsible. List examples of projects you have put off while you have waited for just the right time. How did you feel when pressure built up to finish your work? How did you behave?

WRITE SPECIFIC EXAMPLES

GETTING THE JOB DONE

Have you learned how good it feels to complete a job, not because someone is breathing down your neck about it, but because you want to finish it? How does it feel? Give some examples of things you have done recently that have helped you feel good about yourself. How do you feel about the job that you're doing right now of putting your life together again?

WRITE SPECIFIC EXAMPLES

GUILT FEELINGS

Sometimes, we hang onto bad feelings about ourselves in just the same way we hang onto our resentments against others. Feeling guilty can become an important part of our life style, always there to give us another excuse for feeling miserable and behaving irresponsibly. Describe guilt feelings you still have. Is guilt still an important part of your life?

WRITE SPECIFIC EXAMPLES

FREEDOM FROM GUILT

Are you able now to let go of the guilt? Are you learning how important it is not to hate yourself, but to begin respecting yourself? Can you see that respect for yourself is really a basic part of personal growth?

WRITE SPECIFIC EXAMPLES

FEAR

Sometimes we're afraid of specific things — afraid someone will reject us, afraid a plan won't succeed, afraid someone will find us out . . . and sometimes we're afraid in some vague, general way that we are bound to fail, that nothing will work out, that everything is going wrong. Talk about your own fears, the fears that you have right now, the fears that destroy your peace of mind.

WRITE SPECIFIC EXAMPLES

ACCEPTANCE

As acceptance of ourselves grows, so does our acceptance of the world around us. We don't have to be so fearful and defensive, because there's not so much to worry about. We know that we can only do our best, and after that, what will be will be. Are you learning to trust yourself and to trust others too? Do you find yourself being less afraid? Are you doing less manipulating?

WRITE SPECIFIC EXAMPLES

TAKING THINGS FOR GRANTED

Many of us tend to take things for granted when things are going well with us. We sometimes forget the effort, the action and the discipline which finally got things straightened out for us. Complacency and boredom are real dangers to our new ways of living. Can you recall instances when complacency or boredom caused you to slip back into irresponsible ways of behaving?

WRITE SPECIFIC EXAMPLES

BEING GRATEFUL

How do you feel about your new way of life? Do you show your gratitude to those who helped you build a new life? What are some ways you could express your gratitude right now? Can you see how feeling grateful can influence you in a positive way, and help you avoid the pitfalls of complacency, boredom and depression?

WRITE SPECIFIC EXAMPLES

A PLAN FOR LIVING

Having completed your 4th Step Inventory, where are you now in terms of self-awareness and self-acceptance? What is your attitude toward change and growth? Are you committed to making some changes? How do you see Steps 4 and 5 now as part of a 12-Step Program?

To help you get at these important questions, we encourage you to begin making your own plan for living. As a suggestion, try listing some of your defects, the attitudes and behaviors that are causing you the most trouble, and make some plans to deal with these defects. List some of your assets and incorporate them into your plan for personal growth. Perhaps you have hit upon certain daily disciplines that are helpful. What about your new personal program of spirituality?

Write this material down. Try to be as specific in making your plan for living as you were in making your personal inventory. Then live it!